NORSE MAGIC FOR BEGINNERS

---

a thorough introduction to Elder Futhark Runes Reading, Norse Magick Spells, Rituals, Symbols, and Divination for beginners

NORA BLACK

Copyright © [Year of First Publication] by [Author or Pen Name]

All rights reserved.

No portion of this book may be reproduced in any form without written permission from the publisher or author, except as permitted by U.S. copyright law.

Contents

Introduction	IV
1. Nordic Peoples' Religious History	1
2. The History Of Norse Religion Among Nordic Peoples	7
3. Three Categories Apply To The Norse Gods	32
4. Norse Religion Now	91
5. Tools	124
6. Runes DIY	167

Introduction

The history of the Norse people is extensive in the world of myth and legend. Both Christianity and Paganism had a strong influence on their views. They borrowed their traditions from various faiths and assimilated them into their culture. We will examine a variety of Norse traditions in this book, including Yule or Jól, a two-day festival held in late December. From Baldr's passing to Loki being imprisoned by a snake for his part in creating Ragnarok, mythology will be covered. The history of the Norse people is extensive in the world of myth and legend. Their traditions had strong Christian and pagan roots.

They borrowed their traditions from various faiths and assimilated them into their culture. We will examine a variety of Norse traditions in this book, including the Yule or Jól festival, which is held in late December and lasts for two days. Along with mythology, we will also look at Baldr's passing and Loki's snake-bound imprisonment for his part in the creation of Ragnarok. To cast a spell, make an altar first. This is the simplest method. A "hexagon" or "salt" altar is among the most widely used altars for magic operations.

If you want something that feels more empowering, make sure to utilize candles and conscious intent when setting up your altar and before casting your spell. Additionally, you'll need a clear area where you may do spellcasting, either inside your house or outside if it's secure to do so unhindered." The history of the Norse people is extensive in the world of myth and legend. Both Christianity and Paganism had a strong influence on their views. They borrowed their traditions from various faiths and assimilated them into their culture. We will examine a variety of Norse traditions in this book, including the Yule or Jól festival, which is held in late December and lasts for two days. Along with mythology, we will also look at

Baldr's passing and Loki's snake-bound imprisonment for his part in the creation of Ragnarok. To cast a spell, make an altar first. This is the simplest method. A "hexagon" or "salt" altar is among the most widely used altars for magic practice."

Because you need an account to log in and use the website, creating a Facebook account is the best method to get started. Your login information can be either your phone number or your email address. The Norse gods are represented by the symbols in a symbolic way. The Norse have a lengthy history. Both Christianity and Paganism had a strong influence on their views. They borrowed their traditions from various faiths and assimilated them into their culture. We will examine a variety of Norse traditions in this book, including the Yule or Jól festival, which is held in late December and lasts for two days. Along with mythology, we will also look at Baldr's passing and Loki's snake-bound imprisonment for his part in the creation of Ragnarok."

The history of the Norse people is extensive in the world of myth and legend. Both Christianity and Paganism had a strong influence on their views. They borrowed their traditions from various faiths and assimilated them into their culture. We'll look at a lot of the Norse traditions that are still practiced today in Iceland in this book. We'll discover their mystical beliefs and how they relied on the land to live off of for many years. Because you need an account to log in and use the website, creating a Facebook account is the best method to get started. Your login information can be either your phone number or your email address. The Norse gods are represented by the symbols in a symbolic way.

The history of the Norse people is extensive in the world of myth and legend. Both Christianity and Paganism had a strong influence on their views. They borrowed their traditions from various faiths and assimilated them into their culture. We will look at several of the Norse traditions that are still practiced today in Iceland, including those that deal with magic and those that illustrate how the people there have long subsisted by living off the land."

Scandinavian peoples

Many gods were worshipped by the Norse people. The Norse worldview encouraged people to look up at the heavens and reflect on the power of the gods, and as a result, the population was typically tiny. Due to their intense religiosity, the Norse people required the belief in a god in order to carry out every duty that was necessary for survival. Norse people needed to believe that their deity was in charge of all actions taken to achieve their goals if they were to succeed. The mythology of the Norse people permeated many aspects of modern life. Norse mythology's gods weren't well-known for their strength or stoic work ethic. The Norse gods had a relationship with magic since they depended on it to survive and carry out their duties. In order to succeed and lead fulfilling lives, the Norse religion required magic, which gave people an advantage over their gods. Even though the Norse religion required magic, certain gods had more powerful abilities.

Magic was a very important part of the daily lives of the Norse people, who had a deep believe in it. They believed that if the gods were kind and just and desired the best for their people, magic would revive them and allow life to go on as usual. They thought that for this to happen, magic was required. Even so, this assumption might have unfavorable effects.

According to Norse mythology, the gods would require more than simply magic to raise a deceased person from the dead if their body had been consumed by fire. A sacrifice was necessary. As a result, when someone died, neither the gods nor the person's ancestors could access that person's soul. It was in this manner that the sacred fire was made.

In the Norse religion, sacrifices were a crucial component. The gods, in the eyes of the Norse, required something from humans in order to sustain their existence and resurrect them. In order to gain more power, luck, or even happiness, the Norse sacrificed animals to their gods.

Most frequently, sheep, cows, and horses were offered as sacrifices. They were infamous for offering up people like Freya as sacrifices. In the religion of the Norse, human sacrifice was the only kind that was forbidden. In any other religion, this would be frowned upon and utterly unacceptable.

There are numerous types of magic due to the variety in how it is employed and taught. The same knowledge of farming or medicine in pre-technology times is what is referred to as the "magic" required for survival. Religion and the notion of fate or chance are examples of other magics that are crucial to society and culture. By enabling witnesses to recognize offenders, magic plays a crucial role in everyday life and society, including legal systems. Because it was a fundamental component of daily life, magic was central to Norse society.

When we think of a ritual, we frequently picture a circle of sinister characters plotting the destruction of everyone who has ever wronged them, as shown in twisted Hollywood movies. In reality, a ritual is better performed alone, as with the most of the material we have covered here. Of course, this is wholly off target. Since rituals and spells are always personal, it seems sense that conducting them alone is always favored. This is because doing so allows us to obtain a significant amount of isolation. Group rituals, spells, and castings are definitely something you can participate in, but there will always be a lot of questions and a lot of muddled, disorganized answers.

We are here to learn a beginner's guide to the Elder Futhark, spells, rituals, and divination; therefore, we will just be learning the fundamentals. There is a seemingly unending stream of rituals and spells, and practically all of them are modifications of the ones that came before. This is totally acceptable, and it actually happens naturally with anything that has been passed down over generations, especially when there have been periods of time when records weren't preserved.

Chapter 1

Nordic Peoples' Religious History

What is the history of religion among the Nordic peoples?

Honoring gods for blessings they had received was a central theme of early Norse religion. Because he taught people how to survive through sacrifices and offerings, some people think Odin was a significant god. In early medieval Scandinavia, the gods went by a variety of names, but Christianity gradually gained traction under King Olaf I Tryggvason.

Polytheism, or the worship of multiple gods, was prevalent among the Norse. The Nordic people held the view that a balance between good and evil was important. Additionally, they had three primary methods for worshiping their gods. Below are a few of these:

The polytheistic Norse people used sacrificial ceremonies, in which human or animal sacrifices were made in order to honor their gods, as their first form of devotion. For instance, if a woman wanted Odin to bless her husband, she would sacrifice a horse on his behalf. Another illustration is that warriors would kill a prisoner as a sacrifice to Odin in order for their army to win a battle. Animals were frequently sacrificed during these rituals because it was thought that the gods would be happier if they received an equivalent offering. The killing of an animal in honor of the gods is a good illustration of this. If a man desired healthy crop growth and prolific livestock, he would do this. The concept that a creature was sent to Valhalla, the house of the gods, when it died and its body parts were used, explained the significance of sacrifice for the gods. Animals were sacrificed on behalf of people during illness or famine. The majority of an animal's food was not wasted when it was killed and any desirable body parts (such skin) were used, either for human consumption or to feed other animals. An excellent illustration of this is the sacrifice of an animal to Odin. Because the gods were starving, mutton and lamb were given to them. Nordic polytheism placed a great deal of importance on these sacrifice-based religious rituals.

The Norse people have practiced various forms of god worship throughout history. To appease Asgardian deities, they would engage in games and rituals. For instance, farmers who desired fertile crops would engage in a variety of sports, such as skiing or hurling, that they believed would benefit their crops. This benefited them in their agricultural endeavors.

These contests and rituals are frequently a component of age-old festivals that are ceremonial in nature and heavily reliant on music.

These celebrations are intended to offer a setting where people can come together and form relationships with their gods and one another.

The Yule feast, also known as "Midvinterblot," is one instance of this. It was a significant component of Norse culture and custom. During this festival, people, animals, and even food were sacrificed to ward off evil forces.

The Yule festival used to be a time when people would gather and revel with their friends, families, and Loki; however, it is frequently believed that this was simply a time when people got together to sacrifice humans.

Many locations in Scandinavia that have had a sizable Norse population still pay homage to the gods in some fashion today. For instance, the Faroe Islands host a Viking festival every year where people can celebrate their shared roots with their ancestors by singing songs and consuming mead, a type of alcohol, which is the same as the mead consumed in prior ages.

Chapter 2

The History Of Norse Religion Among Nordic Peoples

Scandinavia's Norse population has a long history of being characterized as warlike, ferocious tribesmen who propagated their belief in the Norse gods. They did, however, worship a pantheon of other gods before swearing allegiance to Odin, Thor, and Baldur. In fact, according to academics, the religion practiced by the indigenous of Scandinavia today originated in Central Asia, where nomadic horse herders worshipped over 40 deities with whom they had to share resources, thousands of years ago. These horse herders also brought a set of religious practices that are still widely held by Mongolian people today, which the Nordic people adopted.

The Yamnaya are thought to have been the first to introduce this old religion to the North. Between 4500 and 3000 BCE, the Yamnaya people moved from Kazakhstan to Russia's Eastern Steppes. By the time they reached Hungary, Romania, Moldova, and Ukraine by around 3500 BCE, northern Greece by 3200 BCE, and southern Poland by 3000 BCE, they had gradually migrated both eastward and westward. The migration of Indo-Europeans to Europe, according to many academics, was caused by the Yamnaya peoples.

The Yamnaya people worshiped a pantheon of gods that coexisted alongside humans, giants, mermaids, and celestial beings in heaven as well as on earth. They held the view that these deities needed to be placated with gifts and sacrifices. They engaged in a form of shamanism known as "early shamanism," where shamans performed healing rituals for the gods and spoke with spirits that were revered as gods.

The Yamnaya peoples built thousands of temples to their gods around 3000 BCE, according to ancient Hungarian sites. When the Yamnaya peoples first came to Central Europe, they brought their simple religion with them, and as soon as they made a settlement, they started erecting shrines to their gods. This early method was used at the Slovenian city of Ptuj. The first temple is thought to have been erected there around 4000 BCE. The god whose name translates to "Great Horseman" had a shrine here. A shrine honoring another horseman-god known as the "Sky Father" was established inside the second temple at Ptuj around 1000 B.C.E.

Additional sites show that 5000 B.C.E., thousands of years earlier, the Yamnaya peoples were already constructing shrines to gods associated with hunting, lightning, and wind; gods associated with death and regeneration; fertility goddesses associated with earth, water, and fire; a god who was portrayed as a half-human, half-wolf creature who was the lord of royal power; a moon god who turns into a wolf at nightfall; and female deities The sun goddess, water and fire fertility goddesses, the god of celestial fire, and the god of thunder are among more deities that are represented in artifacts.

The deity of Jastorf culture was revered by the Yamnaya people. This goddess was pictured facing east toward the rising sun, dressed as a person with stag-like antlers. The goddess was also linked to conception, pregnancy, and other earthly ills like disease and death. From southern Germany, Austria, Czechoslovakia, Hungary, and Poland to western Russia (modern-day Ukraine) and central Asia, many locations in Eastern Europe revered this deity (present-day Kazakhstan).

The Yamnaya peoples venerated shamans who conducted ceremonies for their gods and engaged in spirit communication. During their travels and adventures, these shamans conversed with the spirits. The fact that these shamans had strong ties to the gods is significant. They felt that by sending them on a sacred quest, their god had given them strength and authority. Shamanism persisted in use among the Yamnaya peoples until roughly the third century B.C.E. as southern European cultures began to emerge. Later, after the Roman Empire had conquered all of Central Europe, it imposed its religion on the region and encouraged the spread of other faiths, including Roman-Christianity, Judaism, and Mithraism.

Today, a lot of academics think that the Yamnaya people's ancient religion altered and developed into the Germanic faith or religion in Central Europe. According to scholars, the Germanic peoples who invaded Europe took their religion with them. Beginning about 2800 B.C.E., a Germanic tribe known as the Franks started colonizing the area around Paris, France, a few thousand years after the Yamnaya peoples entered Central Europe. From there, they traveled north and west, settling around 500 B.C.E. in northern Germany and southern Denmark. After these Germanic people established their empire, they started building a multitude of temples to their gods around 1400 B.C. E..

What Alterations Occur With The Coming Of Christianity?

Once you've established a rhythm, repeat the following incantation: "(your selected rune) I Nordhri helga ve theta ok hald vorgh." The translation of this is "Hallucinate and hold this sacred stead" in the North. Our forefathers said these words of protection every day, and when we do so today, they give us the same sense of security.

After making your selection, you can choose a different rune, but this time, make sure to select one that has personal or symbolic significance for you. "(Your chosen rune) I Austri helga ve theta ok hald viirdh," can then be said while you face east. Of course, this means the same thing, but with east in place of north and your chosen rune. Please don't interpret this explanation as being condescending in any way; I'm just simplifying it for you without adding any pointless jargon.

Then, facing south, add the rune you just created to the beginning of the incantation, followed by "... I Sudhri helga ve theta ok hald viirdh."

As you make a U-turn toward the west, select your final rune, bring its image to mind, and once more draw the rune with your staff while saying, "(selected rune) I Vestri helga ve thetta ok hald viirdh." In 2020, Thorsson

Beginning Ritual

This is yet another of the most significant but simplest ceremonies. The majority of rituals, once you master the fundamentals, will be extensions of the Ritual for Protection and Peace of Mind. This simply means that setting yourself up for success by focusing on positive thoughts and surrounding yourself with supportive forces can assist your spells and rituals progress in the direction you desire.

You must once more create a complete circle for the Ritual of Beginning. If training outside seems a bit much right now, keep in mind that this can simply be mentally traced with your staff. Hagalaz and Elhaz are recommended once more as your two physical runes to select.

Once this is finished, get ready by clearing your mind and focusing your thoughts, just as we did during the ceremony. If you need to, you might assume the shape of a cross once more and visualize one in front of you. Take your time, as your mental condition is the most crucial factor in all rituals. Face north as you complete each step.

Select a Nordic prayer that speaks to you or your circumstance. The gods that the Norse people prayed to were numerous and varied in meaning and purpose, from Odin to Kvasir. There are several websites with prayer lists for you to choose from, so don't worry if you haven't read any other books. In the reference list, I will include a link to the finest one.

The Creation Of The World

According to Norse (Old Germanic) paganism, the giant known as Ymir, sometimes known as Aurgelmir, Brimir, or Blainn, was the original being from which all the gods and creatures in the Nine Worlds descended. According to legend, Ymir was created from a water droplet that formed when the heat from Muspelheim and the ice from Niflheim came together.

The first generation of the first gods, goddesses, and other mythical creatures were born thanks to Ymir's hermaphroditic body, and they would later give birth to the future generations.

Ve, Vili, and Odin's brothers were among the younger gods that descended from Ymir. The enormous colossus collapsed into their clutches. The Earth, which they named Midgard, was then formed by these three Norse gods. Between

Asgard, the home of the gods, and Hel, the region of the dead, sits this realm, which serves as a bridge.

The ancient traditions and beliefs of Norse Paganism still exist today, but they have been modified to fit into the current era. The first is to stray from one's essential beliefs and give up one's identity in order to survive. If it had, it would have constituted a betrayal of the core tenets and principles of Norse Paganism. Allowing the modern world to express the fundamental principles and values in its own particular manner is the second strategy for adaptation. Asatru has always survived in this way, and they still do. You'll be able to observe that Asatru itself hadn't altered in the slightest when we compare Asatru in the past to Asatru in the present. But it wasn't always like this.

As with any unfamiliar idea or collection of beliefs, Asatru was not readily accepted by the general populace, especially given that it is founded on Norse mythology. In this article, we examine Asatru in its contemporary form, including its origins, current adherents, and other factors.

The Norse Legend's Account Of How The World Was Created

Overview in general

The Asatruars assert that Asatru is a resurrection of the pre-Christian Norse paganism. To completely comprehend the nature of this religion in the modern world, it is important to understand the phrase "revival." The few Norse Pagans who could secretly worship their religion without being discovered were all that was left of Norse Paganism after Northern Europe was converted to Christianity. By the 12th Century, the faith had all but disappeared. Some people choose to rekindle the flame in the latter half of the 20th century by rediscovering their ancestors' pre-Christian beliefs. In other words, Norse Paganism is a resurgence of an ancient religion rather than a recent invention.

Associated with Mythology

When people learn about contemporary Norse paganism, they typically assume that those who practice it are somewhat mistaken, believing in myths and legendary tales. The truth is that while we have advanced in knowledge and understanding enough to see that mythology is false, it doesn't follow that the ideas it represents aren't true. The ideals and realities that huge serpents and global trees stand for are tactile, even though they may not have ever been. Asatruars don't always take the stories they read at face value. They opt to see the stories as a representation of the underlying truth. The Binding of Fenrir is a good illustration.

The gods eventually reached out to the dwarves and they constructed a chain that could not be broken. The chain appeared to be extremely weak and light, but it was actually indestructible. Fenrir questioned why the Gods would give him such a feeble a tie when it was first given to him. He made a good faith request for a god/goddess to put their hand between his jaws to ensure his own safety. Naturally, none of the gods desired to lose a hand. No one but Tyr offered, and when Fenrir discovered he couldn't escape the chain, he bit Tyr's hand off as a punishment.

The myth is entertaining, and the story is compelling despite being made up, but it has no bearing on one's beliefs in any manner. The advantage is found in the central lesson of Tyr's sacrifice, which is as true as birth and death. The deity offered his own hand as a form of insurance for the wellbeing of the other gods. Not only that, but despite having already gained what he wanted—binding the wolf—he also complied with Fenrir's demands.

connection to gods and spirits

The corporeal existence of Odin and the other gods is not accepted by all Asatruars. They consider gods to be spiritual beings who influence people's lives and cultivate their spiritual selves. They lack a distinct physical appearance and possess no distinguishable "abilities." The belief in the Norse gods is essentially not rooted in their physical identity, but in their spiritual identity, which is described in the Eddas and shaped and experienced through each individual's spirit. Of course, one can choose to connect with a god using any method they see fit, but in essence, the belief in the Norse gods is not rooted in their physical identity. Whether it's a human connection or a spiritual connection, as you are aware, we all experience connection in different ways. Since opinions and subjective experiences are involved, it is difficult to define what it means to have a connection with the divine.

There are nine noble virtues.

Nevertheless, a priest may do a modern blóts alone or in a group. It is possible to script or improvise the words used to call a deity into being. Mead or food are frequently offered as sacrifices. The mead is sprinkled on deity statues, the dirt, or the fire, while the food is positioned in front of an altar or tossed into the flames. Depending on what each community deems appropriate, the ritual's intricacies vary. As long as one's heart is in the right place, there isn't a set template for how the ceremony should proceed. By setting aside some food or mead for their chosen deity, heathens who perform daily sacrifices typically engage in a far less formal and ritualized version of blóts.

In order to do Seir, the practitioner would put himself into a trance. This was done in an effort to communicate with the spiritual world. It was mostly employed in the past for divination and the search for undiscovered knowledge. Some people used it to curse friends and foes. Seir has evolved in modern times to include the use of psychoactive chemicals to cause an altered state of consciousness. Even though it is quite similar to shamanism, it is distinct since it is a belief system based in the Nine Realms. Particularly given that contemporary seir practitioners use the ritual to communicate with Norse spirits and embark on contemplative excursions around Yggdrasil. Seir is typically practiced in groups when one practitioner tries to gain knowledge through the spirit realm while the others pose questions for him to answer.

Seir is consequently less common today, at least in its group form. It is impossible to verify whether or not the practitioner received their responses from the spirit world. Many heathens are reluctant to take part in this ceremony because of concern that some may misuse it for their own gain. One's perception of seir and the degree of trust between them and a seir-worker have a significant impact on their views about the rite.

Getting State Recognition: The Journey

the revival's motivating factors

As with every movement, a number of things inspired the Norse Pagan revival. Over ten centuries of being an essential component of Norse culture were followed by Christianity gradually filling the void left by it. There was a clear cultural gap among the Norse people. The spiritual aspect of Norse Paganism was entirely eliminated over time, leaving only the mythology. In search of an explanation for their profound alienation from their culture of origin, many modern individuals went to their past and came across Norse Paganism.

Many others looked to Asatru for direction because it supported their worldview and values or because it gave them the spiritual fulfillment they had been seeking. Last but not least, even though they were not considered to be members of the Norse Paganist society, some of the earliest heathen groups emphasized religion in order to further their right-wing political and ethnic ideas. Along with fostering ties between the Norse and the rest of the world, Asatru aimed to develop ties between the Norse and their ancestors, cultures, and traditions.

Initially Religious Movements

Norse Paganism, as mentioned previously, never had a single ruling body; instead, it was and is now a widely decentralized religion, with numerous organizations motivated by their own interpretations and understandings.

Regulatory Acceptance

Asatru did not become an official religion in Iceland until 1973. A farmer and poet by the name of Sveinbjörn Beinteinsson founded satrarfélagi in 1972, and that was where it all began. Sveinbjörn approached the minister of justice and ecclesiastical affairs, Lafur Jóhannesson, in December 1972 after the group had been established and garnered a limited number of supporters. The minister declined and abruptly ended the meeting, as was to be expected. There are currently two explanations for why he changed his mind. The minister's place of employment in the town center lost power later that day when a thunderstorm struck. He might have interpreted that as a sign, to be honest. Minister Jóhannesson said when questioned that freedom to found any religious group is guaranteed by the Icelandic constitution.

Pantheon of the Norse

Chapter 3

Three Categories Apply To The Norse Gods

Seir, or the ability to discern futures, was the most potent form of magic known to the gods, and it was mostly used by the goddess Freyja of the Vanir. Another set of gods known as the sir, who were more inclined to utilize weapons and raw strength than magic, waged wars against the Vanir out of equal amounts of jealousy, displeasure, and terror of this power. The violence eventually came to an end after wagers were paid as was traditional, and as part of the peace agreement, hostages from one side were surrendered to the other. This means that, as can be seen below, there are more Sir gods than Vanir gods in the pantheon, yet their interconnectedness in myth serves to provide more nuanced narratives and themes.

The Vanir were more closely associated with fertility, magic, and agriculture, whilst the Sir became the more well-known gods associated with power and battle. Asgard is the home of the Sir, while Vanaheim is the kingdom of the Vanir.

'sir Odin'

He is wed to Freyja, a goddess of love and childbirth who is often referred to as

Frigg in some myths. Baldr, Hermod, and Hodor are their three sons. Additionally, he is well-known for being the father of Thor, whose mother is the soil goddess Jör. Due to his other Old English name Woden, Wednesday is the day of the week that is linked with Odin.

Thor

The most popular deity among the Scandinavian peoples before Christianity was the thunder god, who was frequently seen as the champion of the common man. He is related to fortitude, safeguarding people, and storms. Honor, loyalty, and an unwavering sense of duty—three qualities that the Norse people valued most—often surrounded Thor. With his hammer Mjölnir, he had the authority to sanctify and bless religious sites, but in the same vein, he could also use it to wreak havoc. The powerful hammer's dual function mirrors the twin aspects of human existence. The representation of Mjölnir served as a weapon for solitary rebellion against the new God throughout Scandinavia's Christianization. Choosing to wear pendants in the form of a hammer in contrast to the cross was intentional.

In the hierarchy of deities, where warrior and military might play a secondary role, Thor appears to be on the second tier. He is wed to Sif, a golden-haired goddess associated with the ground and agriculture, and is the deity of both violent storms and sunny, fair weather. It's common to think of their union as the holy union of sky and earth.

His two chariot-pulling goats, Tanngrisnir and Tanngnjóstr, as well as his fabled hammer Mjölnir, are familiars.

Loki

It is well known that the god of mischief is both a jötun (giant; occasionally evil, sometimes beneficial). He occupies a highly unusual position within the pantheon and goes against many of the principles that Odin and Thor uphold.

Loki is the child of the goddess Laufey and the giant Fárbauti. He fathered the deity Nif with his wife Sigyn, as well as the underworld goddess Hel, the wolf Fenrir, the enormous snake Jörmungandr, and the giantess Angreboa.

His name is frequently attributed to the most literal translation of "knot" or "tangle," and this may very well be the major source of his influence on the mythological events. He frequently assumes female forms while changing his appearance to confuse or fool people as part of his theme of defying nature. Due to the lack of evidence of worship for this deity, he may not be regarded as a god like his counterparts.

Baldr

Being generally kind and cheery, this particular god plays a significant, positive role in mythology. He is frequently linked to love, peace, and forgiveness, yet scholars disagree about what role he might have in mythology.

At the conclusion of the Viking Age, when poets and skalds (poets who create skaldic poetry) started producing literature through a Christian perspective, his themes of goodness, beauty, and graciousness were more severely developed. The image of him blazing like the sun, having died, and then being raised from the dead illustrates this by eliminating the god's initial propensity for violence from its pagan origins.

The son of Odin and Frigg, Baldr is wed to Nanna. He is Foresti, the god's father. They are both illegible and infrequently mentioned in earlier works, Nanna and Foresti.

Heimdallr

He is described as having excellent eyesight and hearing so he may keep vigilant watch over the worlds. He is known as the god of foresight, keeper of the Bifröst Bridge, and watcher over Asgard. He lives in his high stronghold called Himinbjörd. He is in possession of the Gjallarhorn, a horn used to warn Asgardians of intruders. Many people concur that he is the child of nine women, each of them are one of the nine daughters of the enormous Aegir.

The other deities that make up the Sir are: Vili and Vé, the two brothers of Odin who together make up the Triad of Spirit, Will, and Holiness.

Hnir, who worked with Odin to create man.

Tr, the one-handed deity connected to morality and valor.

The symbol for the moon and sun is Máni and Sól.

Together with his wife Idun, who looks after the fruit tree in Asgard that grants eternal life, Bragi, the bard of Valhalla, is in charge of greeting the warriors who have died into the hall.

This Vanir Freyja

The Asgardian goddess with the highest power is this. She is linked to death, love, sexuality, fertility, seir, and beauty. She shares with her father and brother the honor of being a sir member. Norse women revered her for their feminine demands and customs, especially in regards to the safety and well-being of their families.

She is most frequently shown as a deity personifying the völva who uses seir magic. The goddess is frequently shown to be promiscuous and unfaithful to her spouse, and she frequently exerts control over people around her. She is closely associated with both war customs and the ideal of shamanism and magic since she rules over her field of Fólkvangr and receives half the warriors who perish in battle for her hall.

It's important to note that she and the goddess Frigg are frequently referred to as being the same person in various stories because Frigg is married to the Norse god Odin (Or). About the 10th century saw the beginning of the post-Christian Germanic divide. Consequently, it is reasonable to conclude that the two goddesses eventually fused to form a single entity. Freyja's name, which seems more like a title than a name and comes from the Old Norse term for "lady," is derived.

Freyja is the sister of the god Freyr and the daughter of the god Njorr. With her three sons and two daughters, Hnoss and Gersemi, she is married to Odin. Two male cats that were gifts from Odin pull her chariot as her familiars. She also owns the boar Hildisvni and can transform into a falcon when wearing a cloak made of falcon feathers. Freyja/Frigg mentions Friday as the first day of the week, which is documented as frigdag, or "Frigg's day."

Freyr

This deity is associated with good fortune, the sun, vigor, and sacral kingship. He is renowned as the god who grants serenity and joy to humans. His themes of both sexual and ecological fertility make him a popular god at weddings and harvest festivals. Boars, notably Gullinbursti, the boar who served as Freyr's familiar, were sacrificed to him at weddings, and thus served as the primary allegory for his virility.

He is the deity Freyja's brother and the god Njorr's son. He later marries the giantess Gerr and rules over the realm of Alfheim, which was a chewing toy for him. His magical sword Sumarbrander and his boar Gullinbursti, both of which are capable of independent combat, are his familiars. Additionally, he captains the Skiblanir, a ship that could magically collapse into a carry bag and always sail in fine weather.

Due to the Vanir's tolerance of incest, the deity is believed to have been romantically involved with numerous goddesses, giantesses, and even his own sister Freyja. He shares the same name as his sister Freyja (a woman), which means "lord."

Njorðr

Njorr represents fertility, just as his children Freyja and Freyr. In his beach realm, Nóatn, he also embraces the concepts of prosperity and, most notably, is revered as the god of the oceans and sailing.

He is the main deity of the Vanir, and sadly, we know very little about him because much of the information we have about him comes from the early Viking Era, when he was largely worshipped.

Those Valkyries

It's possible that the way we currently understand the Valkyries—as graceful shieldmaidens who soar into battle alongside their lord Odin and gather the souls of slain soldiers to bring to Odin's hall—is another Christianization and softening of their actual functions from their earliest pagan times. It is discovered that their initial characteristics were much more sinister; they personify the horror of war and at certain points are shown as wearing intestines as belts and utilizing heads as weights.

The goddess Freyja was believed to be the head of the Valkyries since she would take half of the souls of the slain warriors to her fields in Fólkvangr, while the other souls would either be transported to Valhalla by the Valkyries or go to the world of the dead.

Four of the deities and mythical animals who inhabit the nine worlds are the most heavily worshipped. These are:

Odin, also referred to as Woden, is the All-Father and the king of all Aesir and Vanir. The most feared and enigmatic of all the Norse gods, he is also the most revered. He is typically portrayed as a ragged traveller who is obstinately curious despite being the ruler of all Asgard.

Odin is not perfect, despite how consistently kind-hearted he is portrayed in the media. Additionally, he has a dark side. Odin is seen as embodying the ferocity of battle. He has started a great deal of wars.

Thor - Without a question, Thor is the most well-known of all the Germanic Norse gods, and most of his reputation came from contemporary comics, cartoons, and movies. However, the contemporary Thor differs significantly from the Thor of Norse mythology. The similarities end there, other than the fact that he is grumpy and wields the mystical hammer Mjolnir.

The real Thor has red hair and eyes, and he travels in a chariot drawn by two enormous goats. Along with being the deity of the sky and thunder, Asgar is also his protector.

Along with his twin sister Freya, Freyr is probably one of the most adored of all the Norse gods. Freyr also has a special genesis story. Freyr descended from the

Vanir tribe, in contrast to the majority of other Germanic gods.

The Norse revered him as the supreme deity of fertility, agriculture, harvests, wealth, peace, and sexual vigor. He is frequently shown as a big, strong man with long, flowing hair. Since agriculture was so important to the ancient Norse, many people worship Freyr in the hope of always having a plentiful harvest.

She is the Norse goddess of beauty and love, Freya/Freyja, and the twin sister of Freyr. Her reputation as the goddess of fate and destiny is well-known. After their tribal conflict with the Vanir, she and her twin brother Freyr joined the Aesir as honorary members. In accordance with Norse mythology,

Freya had the power to alter people's futures.

Origins

The Norse performed mystical religious ceremonies. It is reported that the Norse used runes and spells in the forest, but not on humans. Used for divination. The Native Americans distanced themselves from major religious traditions to preserve their beliefs. Different tribal communities defended themselves because of their religion. Many religious practices are done, however this is usually done spiritually.

Religion is the most significant aspect of spirituality, although it doesn't always encompass all of it. Humans also use magic religious ceremonies, but this is rare in organized religions. Still, it can be practiced.

People who believe in magic religious rituals can do them at any time, but most do it during dreamless sleep. This is normally done alone or with one or two others, however some do it in front of others.

Most believers in magic religious ceremonies employ sticks and stones from nature.

The Norse religion's practices

The Norse religion includes several ceremonies. Some practices revere gods and heroes; others focus on healing and divination. The Norse favoured animal or bird sacrifices, runes in ceremonies, and charms derived from the land to ward off evil spirits.

Norse religion is divided into two categories: the public cult, which was dominated by massive religious festivals staged in outdoor wooden temples called "hof," and the private cult, which was generally retained within households. The public ritual featured animal killing. At specified seasons or times of year, rituals were held to record natural occurrences like orr's örlög (wanderings), forecast future events, express thanks for previous events, or solve concerns.

Norse sought to be in sync with local nature so they could use local resources. Mostly farmers, a few traces. It was their economic base. In order to ensure that everyone had enough to eat, land was divided into three types: common land, crofts, and Svi (woodland), which formed up half of Iceland. Most appreciated was sole ownership.

In general, Norse people lived in communities, not in solitude. Most houses lacked doors in case a wolf or bear attacked at night. The Norse practiced family farming or household stewardship. It was familyless. Everybody was part of a large clan and worked together. Cows, sheep, and goats were raised. Men hunted and fished while women produced vegetables and wheat. In this period of Norse poverty, inherited land was typically divided into smaller farms.

The economy was built on subsistence farming, not selling surplus produce. This made the Norse self-sufficient and gave them security against agricultural societies.

Vikings in early medieval Scandinavia led a tough yet simple life. The Vikings were warriors and raiders who stole from lands that couldn't defend themselves. As good farmers, they ate well. They ate breads and cakes prepared with barley or wheat and drank milk, mead, or ale from animals they slaughtered on raids.

The Norse were ritualistic. This is seen in the various stories passed down. These anecdotes offered lessons, praise, and dos and don'ts. Some of these legends were from the old Norse religion, and others were merely ordinary tales.

There are early reports of burnings throughout Scandinavia. Tacitus says there was a temple at Nerthus' holy grove on an island in an estuary. Every spring, Nerthus would visit the island by boat, and everything not allowed on her island would burn (including men convicted of various crimes).

Ritual

The Norse magic religion had several rites. Some rituals honored gods and heroes, while others promoted healing and divination. The Norse favoured animal or bird sacrifices, runes in ceremonies, and charms derived from the land to ward off evil spirits.

The Norse used an altar, table, or stone for candles and burned animal skins in the fire.

Native American tribes focused on healing, worshiping their gods and ancestors, and working in their religious rituals. People who required natural healing performed rituals.

Native American rituals used ceremonies to heal others when they were ill or needed help. These rituals used the power of an object like tobacco or dreaming during a ghost-related ceremony.

The Cost

In Norse magic, an animal or bird was killed for the gods as a sacrifice. It fed ancestors and gods. The animals that may be sacrificed were mainly goats or cows that had not been used in war or hunting.

The Native American tribes used ceremonies to repair and safeguard their health. In their religion, these tribes used animal-shaped stones. They used stones to clean and other things. This power over nature could be employed for healing or protection.

Native American tribes focused on healing, worshiping their gods and ancestors, and working in their religious rituals. People who required natural healing performed rituals.

Native Americans employed crystals, rubies, wooden amulets, and ruby beads in spells and charms.

Ceremony

Each year, religious organizations hold many ceremonies. Some are annual or on particular dates. Celebrations, memorials, baptisms, confirmations, weddings, and funerals are examples of ceremonies (and other rites of passages). Each ceremony begins with prayer.

Norrism Today

Norse and Germanic mythology inspired day naming..

How it's used

Tuesday is called after Tyr, the god of war and justice. Odin's Old English name, Woden, is Wednesday. Thor, the thunder god, names Thursday. Venus was Frigga's star in Norse mythology, therefore Friday is called after her. Frigga knew everyone's fate, even after Ragnarok, but she never told. Saturday's name comes from Saturn. Roman mythology made Saturn the god of agriculture. In the Norse pantheon, many gods and goddesses are involved with fertility, farming, and harvesting, therefore it's the only day of the week without a Norse connection.

Many Christian social traditions refer to Norse mythology. Christmas trees, Yule logs, and Easter egg decorating are examples. Perhaps Santa Claus driving his reindeer across the sky echoes the Wild Hunt. A story mentions leaving a sack of hay for Sleipnir during this time. Perhaps this led to leaving cookies, milk, or booze for Santa.

Heresy (what is, magic and clairvoyance)

In an oral culture, it's odd that runes are so important. Defining rune The word denotes a secret or a whisper. A rune is an Old Norse letter. Runes were employed for writing, protection, divination, and spellcasting. Futharks have three varieties, the oldest dating to 100 BCE.

Odin went to tremendous efforts to attain the knowledge and power of runes. Freya, who protects Rainbow Bridge, is reported to have learned from him. Humans learned runes from Heimdall.

Every rune has a group of specific meanings, and if it falls, is spelled backwards, or "merkstave," it's bad. An example: F (pronounced mannaz). Human or mankind. It is: Visit Ingrid Halvorsen's website Runes, Alphabet of Mystery for runic alphabet details.

Runic symbols were used to protect weapons and property. Swords, shields, spears, and knives may have a Tiwaz rune on the handle to assure victory.

Runes were utilized as decorative motifs on highly made vessels or wood carvings. Symbols were constructed of straight lines or edges to ease carving. In rich homes, drinking glasses, dishes, silverware, and linen may contain runic monograms. Letters and their meanings were used to design jewelry and decorate art like vases. The usage of runes in jewelry creation is a wonderful Norse legacy. Body painters and tattoo artists are inspired by Norse designs.

Morals and ethics of pagan

Today, Norse mythology is influencing a revival of heathenry in Scandinavia, Iceland, and the U.S. This revival aims to build a faith tradition rooted in the past but relevant to present demands. Grundy, 2015) God in Flames, God in

Fetters: Loki in the Northern Religions). This has taken several forms: Theodism began in 1976 with Garman Lord.
In following the old gods, he seeks historical authenticity. This isn't about repeating rituals but contextualizing past ideas and applying them to the present environment. Tribalism and hierarchy are key to redeveloping this lifestyle. Wicca is more founded in Celtic than Germanic paganism, yet they share a belief in gods, goddesses, and nature worship. Wicca involves manipulating nature through rituals to obtain power, prestige, love, or anything else. Believers in reincarnation and karma. Asatru is the most influential pagan religion today. It means "believe in the gods" and is growing in the UK, France, USA, South Africa, Europe, and Scandinavia.

It was founded by Icelandic farmer Sveinbjorn Beinteinsson (1924-1993). 1945: He released Icelandic rhymed poems. His voice was resonant and he looked like an ancient Skald. He read his poems and Edda sagas at public events. His recordings can be obtained online. Iceland became a national religion in 1973, followed by Denmark and Norway.

The priest is Hilmar Orn Hilmarsson. In 2015, they opened the first modern Norse temple. It's at Thingvellir Park near Reykjavik. Asatru communities are called Kindreds and meetings are called Blots. Mead, a honeyed wine, beer, or cider, is consecrated to a god and the rest is poured forth as a libation to that god. A Sumbel is a toast in three rounds. The first toast is to Odin, the second to ancestors and the dead, and the third is for anyone.

The adherents value courage, truth, honor, fidelity, discipline, hospitality, industriousness, self-reliance, and perseverance. If one lives with these values, the afterlife will bring "more fulfillment, joy, and challenge." If one lives improperly, they will be "separated from family and live in gloom" in the hereafter. Daily, the movement gains greater formal recognition. Heathen and Asatru have been added to the U.S. Army and Air Force's religious preferences list. Asatru Folk Assembly was created by Stephen McNallen in 1994 as a result of neo-Nazi membership strife in the Asatru Free Assembly. Asatru Free Assembly membership is based on bloodlines;

they condemn racism but only accept those of proven Germanic origin.

Modern paganism

To comprehend the Norse Faith practices, one must first understand its purpose, which is to make sure that society survives and regenerates. Because of this, neither the Old Norse religion nor Modern Norse Paganism has standardized rituals and practices, although there are shared elements between congregations.

The Cornerstones Of The Norse Religion In Our Time

The Old Norse had several hátíðir (celebrations), and while they tended to vary between regions, but there were a few major ones for all of them.

Life Transitions were also greatly celebrated.

Blot And Symbel (Sumble)

Blót translates as "blood." The word "blessing" comes from the Anglo-Saxon "blétsung," which meant "sprinkle with blood," so a Blót often involved animal sacrifices which were usually farm animals like pigs and horses.

Blót, for the Old Norse, was the main way to have communal worshipping rituals and was also the source of Veizla, the sacred communal feast.

In a traditional Blót, the sacred animal would be presented to the Blót participants where they would have the chance to lay hands on it and express gratitude for its death and the sustenance it would provide to the people while relaying messages to the gods. The animals were treated with the utmost reverence and respect during its life. Participants of the Blót had to be calm and collected so as not to alarm the sacrificial beast. The death should also be fast and clean, ensuring the least suffering possible for the beast. The blood would be collected in a sacrificial bowl, the hlautbolli, and would then be used to sprinkle the Blót participants, using a branch of evergreen or some other plant.

The Altars

A spoiled Blót would be rejected by the gods and would bring ill luck upon the participants.

Modern Pagans sometimes choose to perform actual Blót with sacrificial animals. However, some groups and organizations either do not wish to do so or are not allowed to do so due to regional restrictions. These adherents usually perform a symbolic Blót using sanctified mead instead of blood.

Seasonal holidays can vary from faction to faction. Still, Scandinavian and Icelandic Norse Pagans tend to place emphasis on Thórr's Day, Winternights, and Jól, which are one of the few Old Norse holidays of which we have knowledge. The Old Norse people were quite busy with their crops during the warmer seasons and had to stay inside during the long dark winters, resulting in fewer holidays during warm-weather times.

Rituals In Our Time (In Groups Or Alone, And At Home)

Some deities have special days dedicated to them, while others, such as Loki, aren't tied to specific times of the year.

According to Snorri Sturluson, there were three major hátíðir in pre-Christian Scandinavia and Iceland. They are also the three Blót that were celebrated by almost all adherents.

Sigrblót (Victory Blót) The festival celebrating the beginning of summer

Winternights (Vetrnætr), which celebrated the beginning of winter, usually in the middle of October, and has been connected to Dísablót

Midwinter (most likely Jólablót or Yule) that takes place on the Winter Solstice.

Midsummer was also an important Blót which was celebrated on the summer solstice, as the name suggests. As Nordic sentiments traditionally recognized only two seasons, summer and winter Jólablót and Miðsummer Blót were considered Greater Hátíðir.

Miðsummer Blót

This is a traditional major festival to honor summer. Even though Sturluson didn't mention Miðsummer, it appeared in the writings of a Winchcombe monk close to Gloucestershire.

The Miðsummer Blót is usually celebrated on June 21st on the summer solstice, which is the longest day of the year. It is often associated with the death of the gleaming Baldr, as the day begins shrinking after this day.

The Divinatory Practice Of Northern Europe Called "Seidh" Is Being Rediscovered

According to the Old Icelandic calendar, the beginning of the Icelandic summer falls around the end of April, and it is still celebrated in the country as a national holiday. It is also the day that Norse Pagans (and Ásatrúarfélagið in particular) celebrate Sigrblót, the victory sacrifice.

The laws that Óðinn established were written down in the Ynglinga Saga and included a statement about when the three majors Blót of the year should be made.

"A sacrifice shall be made when we're coming to winter so as to have a good year. In the middle of winter, there should be a sacrifice for a good harvest, and then the third in the summer, which will be a victory sacrifice."

The connection of the Ásatrúarfélagið branch with the Norse faith, apart from the holiday, also celebrates its founding in 1972.

The celebration can be treated as a victory against the harshness of winter, which traditionally has been seen as life winning against death.

Pagan Rituals Today (Together Or At Home)

Countless blades of grass and other kinds of plants begin to sprout from a ground that until very recently had been frigid and unwelcoming. Migrating birds return home. Farm animals welcome their newborns at this time of the year. Life has won!

For people in countries like Iceland and Scandinavia, with winter being so long and dark, especially close to the Arctic Circle, the arrival of summer tends to be far more important than people living in sunny countries all year round.

However, the element sigur from which sigr in Sigrblót comes doesn't necessarily need to mean victory. It can also take the meaning of accomplishment, success, result, and advantage. Furthermore, the passage in Ynglinga Saga where Sigrblót is mentioned doesn't say anything about military victory, ships embarking or raiding, so it could literally be applied to anything for which one would wish success.

Runic Talismans And The Chanting Of Spells (Galdor)

Winternights or Vetrnaetr (Old Norse for Winter Nights) is a Norse festival that takes place in winter. It was at first celebrated in Iceland and Scandinavian countries before their Christianization. Dísablót has also often been associated with Winternights and is an old hátíð in honor of the Dísir.

It is one of the three most important celebrations for Norse Pagans and marks the beginning of winter and the new year as well as the end of summer. It is customary to perform a Blót to thank the gods for bountiful summer and to ask for protection during the long and harsh winter. The time varies according to the region's weather, but it is usually celebrated in the middle of October, usually four weeks following the autumn equinox.

Many deities were honor during Winternights, among whom were also the álfar.

There were large pits with cauldrons over heated stones where they would boil meat indoors or outdoors. As stated in the Heiðreks Saga, a woman would smear the blood of the sacrifice on an altar, or the statues of the deities, on the participants of the Blót, and on the walls of the building if indoors. That was because it was believed to have special powers.

The adherents gathered around the cauldrons and would feast with their gods and the álfar. They also shared a drink, which was usually mead or beer, which was passed around from person to person, as a symbol of unifying the community.

They would toast to a good year and peace, "til árs ok friðar," and would also ask for the New Year to bring health, life, and harmony between the people and the gods.

Modern Winternights

Most hearths prefer to focus their Winternights celebrations around the dísir and the álfar. A potluck dinner is often arranged based on Old Norse recipes or foods, and a Sumble might be held in honor of the ancestors and people that might have passed in the year that is ending. That can involve both humans and pets and is usually followed by a dinner and a toast.

Jólablót

Jól is possibly the most significant holiday of the year. Like most other Blót or rituals, Jól is deeply rooted in the change of seasons. It's when the sun is reborn. The winter solstice is on the 21st of December, usually the day on which the Jólablót is celebrated. Darkness prevails in the world as this is the longest night of the year. However, after it passes, the day begins to steadily gain more ground, bringing with it the return of the sun and the light.

The winter solstice is often associated with rebirth, as the sun returns after the darkness to spread light and help the crops grow. It signals the arrival of warmer, brighter times, assuring that the sun and the warmth will be once again there to provide people with motivation, joy, and strength, bringing on the rebirth of the soul as well.

People gathered to celebrate the end of winter, oaths taken at the beginning of the year were renewed, and people thanked the spirits of the land, their ancestors, and their gods. In the darkness of the longest night, fires burned hot and bright, in their homes and their hearts.

The festival was largely dedicated to Óðinn, who rides with the Wild Hunt on the day of the Solstice. The night before the Jólablót is known as Modraniht

(Old Norse for "Mother Night"), and it is common to make a toast to Frigg the Allmother, as well as the other female deities and important women in a Heathen's life. Modraniht kickstarted the celebrations at the sunset of the Solstice. The celebrations would last for twelve nights, during which Óðinn, the Allfather, would visit Midgard along with the spirits and ancestors to give gifts to the humans. It was a celebration about family and friend connections and to consider the deeds of the year. It was also about being determined to make the next year an even better one.

The Wild Hunt was called Odens jakt in Old Norse, meaning Óðinn's hunt, or Oskoreien (The Terrifying Ride), or Asgårdsreien ("the Asgard Ride"). The hunt would be heard but very rarely seen, and a usual sign was that of one of Óðinn's dogs barking lowly while the other barked loudly. When the hunt was heard, it would mean that the weather would change, but it could also mean war or unrest.

The Hunt would travel through the forests while winds and storms swept and howled over the world. Nobody wanted to be caught outdoors during that time, for if the Hunt spotted anyone, they would either have to join the Hunt or be carried away and left far from where they had been.

Modern Jólablót

For the modern Norse Pagans, Jól celebrations start with the Jólablót, which is performed outdoors. During the ritual, adherents gather around a candle fire in a circle and listen to stories about Freyr and how he fell in love with the Jötunn Gerður and went to great lengths and made sacrifices to win her over as his partner. During the darkest hours of the year, Freyr falls in love with Gerður, who is like a token of the sun, light and beautiful. When she agrees to marry him, the sun starts to rise once more, bringing along the promise of better days.

After the story, adherents can gather to share a drink from a drinking horn and feast on the traditional smoked lamb or Hangikjöt (hanging meat), Icelandic smoked meat that is usually boiled and can be served hot or cold. It is traditionally served sliced, with potatoes covered with béchamel sauce or green peas. After the feast, the children make a sun out of the candles and then receive small presents. There might also be entertainment, like music performances.

Fórn

A Fórn was a sacrifice of a more materialistic nature. The word is still used in modern Icelandic ("Fórn") (n. fem.) "Fórna" (v.), which means "sacrifice" and "to sacrifice").

The sacrificed items of a Fórn consisted of anything having to do with material wealth, from weapons and jewelry to food and tokens. When one gave a Fórn, the offering had to be destroyed or otherwise rendered useless for mortals. The most common methods to do that were burying, immolation, or shattering of the offering. Sometimes a Fórn was done along with a Blót or as an addition to it. Sometimes an effigy (called "mock sacrifice") could be called a Fórn.

Veizla

A "Veizla" was a feast that was done either in honor of a person or in honor of a deity. It always followed a Blót or a Fórn, and as mentioned, in the case of a Blót, the sacrificial beast's meat was used for the main course.

The hosts of a Veizla would always be seated at the head of the table, and they would usually make a toast during the feast to whomever they were honoring.

By partaking in a Veizla and eating the flesh of the sacrificial beast, one should remember they are consuming part of its essence and power, along with the essence of the gods honored during the

Blót. A Veizla custom involves leaving a part of the feast outside for the land spirits. Sometimes a place was set at the table for the ancestors so that they could also have their share of the revelries.

Sumble/Bragarfull

The Sumble is originally a Saxon ritual that Modern Norse Pagans have adopted. It is what usually comes after the Veizla, and it is as much a ceremony as the rest of these events. Tacitus, in particular, mentioned this ritual in "Germania" with a remark about how amazing it was that the tribesmen would just air their personal matters before everyone in their community. Sumble is also mentioned in several other literary works such as Heimskringla, Beowulf, and the Jómsvíkinga saga.

Tradition holds that any boast, oath, or toast uttered during a Sumble will go straight into the Well of Wyrd and will be heard by the gods. Words spoke during a Sumble must be taken seriously at all times since each participant affects the Wyrd for ill or for good.

Sumbles were always performed in a closed hall to ensure that the event would remain sacred and separated by everyday life and that it was taking place outside space and time. That way, participants would feel a connection to gods and ancestors, as well as the spirit world.

Three positions occur in a Sumble apart from being a simple participant. Those are the Drighten, Thule, and Valkyrie.

The Drighten is the one who is in charge of the Sumble. They declare the beginning of the Sumble, as well as the beginnings and endings of rounds.

The Thule is the one who guards the luck of the kindred and the hall. The Thule's task is to challenge any oath or boast that might poorly affect the luck of the kindred or might potentially be offensive to the gods. If a Sumble participant is challenged, they get the chance to re-affirm their oath or boast and are allowed to call upon someone present in support so that they can speak for them. However, no one should be offended if they're challenged as the

Thule's only concern is to safeguard the örlög (destiny) and luck of the group.

If the challenged one doesn't complete his oath or his boast is false, then by challenging him, the Thule notes that the group has notified the Gods, so the sole blame falls on the challenged and not on the group.

The Valkyrie should be a woman. However, it doesn't matter if one isn't available. She is the one who blesses the drink and is the one who must at least pour the first horn-full of drink. That is because women were believed to have magical properties of nourishing and healing

Sumbles are usually dedicated in distinct ways, depending on the content of the rounds. Usually, the first one is for the gods and the spirits, the second round is for the heroes and the ancestors, and the third is most commonly an open round for the oaths, boasts, and toasts. There might be more rounds after the third, which usually involve feats of song, poetry, etc.

At the end of each round, the remainder of the drink is poured in a hlautbolli. Some is collected in a ladle from the bowl and poured back into the drinking horn, the horn is refilled with more blessed drink, and the rounds continue. This way, the gods, the ancestors, and the mortals share drinks.

No matter the number of rounds, it is important to remember these things:

A Sumble is a sacred ritual, and the atmosphere should be preserved as such and not devolve into a simple party.

It is considered improper not to give one's full attention to whoever is holding the drinking horn during a Sumble.

Interruptions, commentary, and starting irrelevant conversations or shouting are considered very rude.

Getting drunk at Sumble is also considered quite rude.

Participants should pay attention to all toasts and say "Hail" when one drinks.

If a participant can't communally drink from the horn for any reason, then they may kiss the side of the horn. No one will consider it odd or strange in any way.

The Bragarfull is the Scandinavian equivalent, meaning "promise-cup," "chieftain's cup," or "best cup" used to be a ritual where people would drink from a cup or a drinking horn during ceremonies and would swear oaths while the cup was imbibed by a chieftain or was being passed around to those assembled.

Runes Old And New

This is an old notion that described how ancient individuals had distinct names in different societies. Internationalization Every culture has its own philosophy of life, and some theories deem these norms "natural" for a given set of people.

In ancient times, cultures on opposite parts of the globe had similar spiritual/religious ideas. Some had the same beliefs and customs. Some shared similar views on how to handle women and men. Some believed in gender equality... To understand Norse Faith, one must first realize its purpose: sustaining and rebuilding society. Neither Old nor Modern Norse Paganism have standardized rites and traditions, yet there are similar components.

Chapter 4

Norse Religion Now

The Old Norse had various hátir (celebrations) that differed by location.

Honoring life changes.

Blot/Symbel (Sumble) "Blessing" stems from Anglo-Saxon "blétsung," which meant "sprinkle with blood." A Blót often involved animal sacrifices, usually pigs and horses.

Old Norse used Blót for worship and Veizla for a feast.

In a traditional Blót, attendees would touch the sacred animal to express gratitude for its death and the sustenance it would provide while conveying messages to the gods. Blót participants had to be calm so as not to scare the sacrificed animal. Animals should die quickly and cleanly to reduce suffering. Blood from a sacrifice bowl, the hlautbolli, was used to sprinkle Blót participants with a branch or plant.

Ashes

Unspoiled Blót is cursed by the gods.

Modern Pagans sacrifice animals in Blót. Some groups and organizations can't due to geography. They do a symbolic Blót using sacred mead.

group holidays vary. Scandinavian and Icelandic Norse Pagans celebrate Thórr's Day, Winternights, and Jól, an Old Norse holiday. The Old Norse were busy with crops during the summer seasons and had to stay inside during the long dark winters, resulting in fewer holidays.

Rites Now (In Groups Or Alone, And At Home)

Loki has no holy days.

Snorri Sturluson said Scandinavia and Iceland had three hátir. Everyone honored these three Blót.

Sigrblót is a summer festival. Winternights (Vetrntr) marks the advent of winter in October and is related to Dsablót Midwinter (most likely Jólablót or Yule) on the Winter Solstice.

Blót was also held on the summer solstice. For the Nordics, Jólablót and Misummer Blót were Greater Hátir.

Heat wave

Summer's celebration. Sturluson never mentioned Misummer, but a Winchcombe monk did.

Misummer Blót is on June 21, the summer solstice. After Baldr's death, the days grow shorter.

Seidh is a Northern European divination tradition.

Old Icelandic calendar summer begins in April and is still a holiday. Norse Pagans celebrate Sigrblót, the victory sacrifice.

The Ynglinga Saga provides inn's laws about when to make the three big Blót.

As winter nears, we must sacrifice for a productive year. Winter should have a harvest sacrifice, and summer a triumph sacrifice.

The branch also honors its 1972 founding.

The celebration marks life's victory over winter's death.

Rituals (Together Or At Home)

Grass and other plants rise from a chilly, unwelcoming ground. Migration ended. Farm animals give birth in spring. Success!

In Iceland and Scandinavia, where winters are long and dark, summer is more important than in sunny places year-round.

Sigrblót's element sigur doesn't always mean triumph. It can also indicate benefit and result. The Ynglinga Saga passage about Sigrblót doesn't mention military triumph, ships, or raids, so it might refer to anything successful.

Vetrnaetr (Old Norse for Winter Nights) is a winter Norse festivity. Iceland and Sweden celebrated before Christianity. Dsablót is a Dsir Winternights hat.

It marks the onset of winter, the new year, and the end of summer. A Blót praises the gods for a prosperous summer and prays for protection through the difficult winter. It's usually around October, four weeks following the autumn equinox.

Winternights honor álfar.

Large pits with cauldrons over hot stones boiled meat indoors or out. In the Heireks Saga, a lady spilled sacrifice blood over an altar, deity sculptures, Blót participants, and indoor walls. It had unusual powers.

Adherents feasted with their gods and the álfar in cauldrons. They passed mead or beer to show togetherness.

They'd toast a good year and peace, "til árs ok friar," and pray for health, life, and harmony with the gods.

Winter Nights

Winternights celebrates the dsir and the álfar. A potluck lunch of Old Norse dishes or delicacies is often held, and a Sumble is done to remember ancestors and recent deaths. It's followed by a meal and toast for humans and pets.

Jólablótjól is a holiday. Jól is a seasonal Blót, like others. Reborn sun Jólablót is on December 21, the winter solstice. The longest night is universal darkness. After it passes, day brings sun and light.

The winter solstice marks the return of the sun after the darkness to spread light and cultivate crops. It signifies the arrival of warmer, brighter times, bringing soul rebirth with the sun and warmth.

People celebrated the end of winter, reaffirmed oaths, and praised land's spirits, ancestors, and gods. During the longest night, houses and hearts were ablaze.

Inn, who rides with the Wild Hunt on Solstice, was honored. On Modraniht (Old Norse for "Mother Night"), before

Jólablót, Heathens toast Frigg the Allmother and other female deities and significant women. Modraniht celebrated solstice sunset. Inn, the Allfather, visited Midgard with spirits and ancestors to bestow gifts to humans. It was a day to enjoy and reflect on the year. It's also about making next year better.

Old Norse termed it Oden's jakt, inn's hunt, Oskoreien, or Asgrdsreien. One of the inn's dogs gently barked as the other barked loudly. A hunt could signal a weather change, war, or instability.

The Hunt went through forests while storms raged. No one wanted to be outdoors then because if the Hunt noticed them, they'd have to join or be hauled away.

Modern Norse Pagans start Jólablót with Jól. During the ceremony, believers congregate around a candle fire and listen to stories about Freyr and how he fell in love with Jötunn Gerur and made sacrifices to win her over. Freyr falls in love with Gerur at the darkest hours of the year. The sun rises when she accepts to marry him.

After the story, followers can drink from a drinking horn and consume hot or cold smoked lamb or Hangikjöt. Traditionally, it's served with potatoes, béchamel, or green peas. After feasting, kids construct a candle sun and get gifts. Music may be played.

Fórn

Materialist A Fórn. Modern Icelandic uses "sacrifice" ("Fórn" (f.) "Fórna" (v.)).

Fórns gave weapons, jewelry, food, and tokens. If you gave a Fórn, you had to destroy it. Offerings were buried, burned, or shattered. A Blót might have a Fórn. Fórn is a sacrifice effigy.

Veizla

A "Veizla" was a person or god's feast. Always followed a Blót or Fórn, and a Blót's flesh was the main entrée.

Veizla hosts sat at the front of the table and toasted honorees.

By consuming a Veizla and the sacrifice beast's flesh, one eats its essence and power along with the Blót gods. Land spirits are fed part of the Veizla feast. Ancestors sometimes have a seat at the table.

Sumble/Bragarfull

Norse Pagans adopted the Saxon Sumble. It's as ceremonial as Veizla. Tacitus in "Germania" was amazed that tribesmen would air personal concerns in public. He's in Heimskringla, Beowulf, and Jómsvkinga.

Tradition believes every boast, oath, or toast spoken at a Sumble is heard by the gods. Each Sumble participant affects the Wyrd.

Sumbles were usually held in a closed space to keep the ceremony sacrosanct. So, participants feel connected to gods, ancestors, and spirit realm.

A Sumble user has one of three roles. Valkyrie, Thule, and Drighten

Sumble is run by Drighten. Sumble and round begins and stops are announced.

The Thule defends clan and hall's luck. Thule's task is to question any oath or boast that harms the kindred or offends the gods. If challenged, Sumble participants might reiterate their oath or boast and call on a supporter to speak for them. No one should be insulted if they're challenged, as the Thule only care about örlög and luck.

The Thule emphasizes that if the challenger doesn't complete his pledge or his brag is dishonest, the group has told the Gods, therefore the burden falls on the challenged.

Female Valkyrie Then it's irrelevant. She blesses the first sip horn. Women were supposed to have healing powers.

Sumbles depend on rounds. The first round is for gods and spirits, the second for heroes and ancestors, and the third for oaths and toasts. After the third round, add song, poetry, etc.

Each round's leftover drink goes into a hlautbolli. A portion of the bowl's drink is ladled into the drinking horn, which is refilled. The gods, ancestors, and mortals drink it.

No matter how many rounds, remember that a Sumble is a ritual.

It's rude to ignore the Sumble drinker.

Disruptions, comments, and irrelevant conversations are rude.

Being drunk is disrespectful.

Say "Hail" when someone drinks.

Those who can't drink from the horn can kiss it. It's not weird.

The Bragarfull, meaning "promise-cup," "chieftain's cup," or "best cup," was a ceremony where participants drank from a cup or drinking horn at rituals and made vows while the cup was imbibed by a chieftain or passed around.

As of today, democratic laws are not "natural". At the same time, gender equality has become more accepted. This law isn't implemented in all countries. Some "democratic" countries believe being female or male is a state of being. To have many female or male names that have no real meaning yet indicate personalities. Although it's normal for this society to have life philosophy they assume as a given.

Origin of Runes

Runes were utilized in Scandinavia in the 2nd and 3rd centuries AD. One of Europe's earliest types of writing.

Also termed futhorc (fewer than 30 samples preserved), this paper is considered a not-quite-finished written language. The runes date to at least 200 AD, but academics disagree on what they mean. There are no translations for these texts, so specialists can't tell if they are religious or if they are a secret code for ancient people who didn't want visitors to know their words.

The runes symbolize earth's power and shape. They also represent a writing system, but it's unknown what they say or who made them. Over 300 runes from the 2nd century BC were created near the end of that period.

Early types of writing featured more than 2,000 spells, including some that tell old legends (hundreds or thousands of years before these illustrations). On 910-915 AD, Harald Hardrada (Harald Fairhair) carved the first 18 runes in stone and wood. The oldest runic inscriptions in Scandinavia.

It's the oldest form of writing in Europe. Many use them to show love, loyalty, and wisdom. Not all rune meanings are given in the texts, but there is a lot of curiosity about their history and mysteries.

Today, runes are widely used in private writings (such as love letters) and weddings. During the Iron Age, people would write their names on old rune stones as a magical charm to protect them from evil spirits or spells. These letters are used to type common phrases on a computer keyboard.

From the Vikings to today, a history of runes

The idea of sacrificing something important to the main character in exchange for knowledge and power is common in Norse mythology sagas and poems. True sacrifice was self-sacrifice. The original theme is in Hávamál from the Poetic Edda, which shows Odin's struggle from his own perspective.

The great Odin is hungry for all wisdom. He sacrifices his eye and throws himself on his spear, Gungnir, to find this mighty wisdom at Mmir's Well. Here, he receives half the knowledge he needs, so he continues to search.

From Asgard, he sees the Norns below Yggdrasil weaving the fates of all beings. So Odin decides to learn their magic, but he must again sacrifice something to do so. So, self-wounded by a spear, he hangs in a tree for nine days and nights, looking into the pool and refusing help from the other gods.

I hung on a wind-rocked tree for nine nights, spear wounded, and offered myself to Odin on that tree, whose root no one knows.

No one gave me bread or drink;
I peered downward, studied runes, learned them, and fell. 138th verse of Hávamál

Finally! Visions and secrets revealed runes to him. But he's changed and reborn. Half of Odin's self-died in that tree, and he emerged stronger, symbolizing passing the physical limits of the mortal self to reach the divine and immortal.

He then passes on the runes to the men of the world so they can learn and grow like he did.

Myths aside, historical evidence shows that Germanic tribes often warred and traded with Romans in the south and brought back to Scandinavian kingdoms their own take on the Old Italic language, molding and altering it to their own worldview, thus creating the Elder Futhark.

The Runic Alphabet (Futhark) is the original and oldest Scandinavian language, appearing in the 1st century during the Dark Ages.

The name Futhark comes from the first six letters of their alphabet.

- fehu - naubiz - ehwaz - uruz - isa - mannaz - burisaz - jera - laguz - ansuz - eihwaz - inguz - raido - perb -

Since the names in these runes are not preserved in Elder Futhark, historians must reconstruct them from later runic alphabets, almost like retracing steps of language. Gothic is the earliest available Germanic language in large cohesive texts from 300 C.E., when the letter names were based on runes.

The Anglo-Saxon (Old English) texts created the Anglo-Frisian Futhorc in the 5th century. This version, with 24 to 33 characters, was used by Frisian cultures and brought to England via manuscripts.

It was replaced by the Latin alphabet in the late 11th century.

Although rare in the Viking Age, bind-runes were used to bind two or more runes. They were either a simple two rune (rarely three) combination to make a glyph. Then, the same-stave rune, a larger conglomeration of runes, appeared on runestones.

You can write it as a direct letter for rune translation, which may not be how it's pronounced (but how it's spelled), or you can write it phonetically, which removes or changes runic letters accordingly. There are no runic letters for all 26 English letters or sounds.

Teen Futhark

In the 7th century, 8 of the 24 Elder Futhark characters were removed.

It created the 16-character Younger Futhark of the Viking Age, also called the Scandinavian Futhark.

Vowels were added and characters removed, changing the language. Thus, a trend toward a more minimalistic and useful form of the language where diplomatic and trade-oriented subjects can be expressed. Some sounds were spelled the same.

- Fé - Hagall - Bjarkan - r - Naur - Mar - Thurs - Is - Logr - As/Oss - Ar - Yr - Rei - Sol - Kaun - Tyr

The Younger Futhark split into long-branch Danish runes, which were better for stone, and short-twig (Rök) runes, which were used for personal messages on wood. Swedish and Norwegian origin.

Some runes lacked the strokes and lines of the Younger Futhark. These runes were called Hälsinge Runes or staveless runes because they lacked a stroke—a "budget rune."

Rune poems are the most relevant source for the 16-letter Younger Futhark alphabet. They explain each runic letter in a poetic stanza to help with pronunciation and relevance. Each rune poem has a few lines with memorable images to help remember the rune.

They're divided into Norwegian, Icelandic, and Anglo-Saxon. Norwegian and Icelandic poems use the Younger Futhark, while Anglo-Saxon uses the relevant Runic alphabet.

Due to the amount of information on each version of the poems, we will provide the most systematized: the Icelandic Rune Poems of the 15th century.

Source of discord among kinsmen ok flar viti, fire of the sea ok grafseis gata, path of the serpent aurum fylkir.

Lament of the clouds (ok skára verrir), ruin of the hay harvest (ok hiris hatr), and abomination of the shepherd.

UmbreVISI

urs is a crow

Torturer of women ok kletta bi and cliff-dweller ok varar verr.

- As/ss (God)

ss is old

Gautr ok ásgars jöfurr, lord of Valhalla and prince of Asgard.

- (Riding)

The horsemen's joy

Good luck, Jórs erfii!

and horsework.

Kaun (Ulcer) is a fatal disease for children ok bardaga för and a painful spot ok holffa hs.

and mortuary

- Hagall (Hail) Hagall is the king's flag.

Cold grain, krapadrfa, and sleet, snáka sótt.

venomous snakes

Grando Hildingr

- Naur (Constraint)

ungr kostur and vássamlig verk are the bone-grief maid's and oppression, respectively.

hard work

Opera Niflungr

- s er árbörkr

Bark of rivers ok unnar ak, wave roof ok feigra manna fár.

the doomed's destruction

- r er gumna gói.

Good summer to men and algróinn akr.

growing crops.

annus allvaldr - Sól

Shield of the clouds okay?

rota siklingr's shining ray.

And icebreaker

God with one hand ok ulfs leifar and leaving of the wolf ok hofa hilmir.

king of temples

Mars tiggi. - Bjarkan

Itit tré means leafy twig and ingsamligr vir means little tree.

new shrub.

- Mar Mar er manns gaman

Delight of man ok moldar auki and enhancer of the earth ok skipa skreytir.

- Lögr (Water) Lögr is vatn

Eddying stream ok vir ketill and broad geysir ok glömmungr grundi.

r (Yew) r bendr bogi

Giant of the arrow ok brotgjarnt járn, brittle iron ok ffu fáarbauti.

Here, each poem relates to the theme and character of a rune. Like singing rhymes to children to teach English and word association, this was used to learn and remember. The first syllable's stress makes it hard to relate to modern English. Norse poetry alliterates the first letter of a word, while English uses the last letter.

Using runes

With Norse settlement in Iceland around 870 C.E., the Younger Futhark alphabet was adapted for magical purposes. This is a group of characters combining their powers. You'd find three or more runes combined into an intricate character with magic and meaning.

Galdrasafur, meaning "magical stick" or "stave," was used by men in Iceland. They were carved on specific materials like other Nordic runes and had a certain effect. Small drops of blood were also sacrificed to the magic. Very specific to what the Icelanders needed at the time, their magic was used to kill an enemy's cattle, increase fertility, "guide through bad weather or bring victory during wrestling, called glma," and more (Iceland Rovers, 2017). Some were used for fishing or rowing, healing fox bites, or making sheep docile.

In the 16th century, the outlaw of runes was heavily enforced, and many men were executed for still practicing their pagan religion and using runes at home.

Aegishjálmur, "Helm of Awe," was shaped like a four or eight to form a cross with branches. In this saga, Sigurd slays the great serpent Fáfnir to win a Niflung treasure horde. Part of the treasure is Aegishjálmur's symbol, which gave him power and protection. Solomons Innsigil was renamed after Christianity took hold.

A unni, a simplified version of Aegishjálmur with fewer branches, was a love stave. So a man may find a woman. This symbol was drawn with right-hand spit.

The Hraethigaldur is a scary stave. Carved on bark and worn as a pendant, this would scare your enemies. See your enemy before he sees you. Rune divination

The purpose of runestones was to be seen. They are large upright slabs of stone with messages, poems, and life stories about the person or family. The runes were often painted with bright colors and elaborate drawings of battle or triumph. Both men and women commissioned runestones to boost their social status in the community. Most of the runestones still standing today are in Sweden, but many more can be found in Denmark, Norway, and other places Vikings raided and traded.

Inscriptions on large stones and bedrock began in the 4th century and lasted until the 12th century, when the Viking Age ended.

Most runestones were carved by Norse converts in the Viking Age. This was likely to show neighbors how well they had converted to Christianity and abandoned their pagan past.

Chapter 5

Tools

Runes needed to be carved correctly and placed on the right surface and location to invoke the right deity for their purpose. Bad luck and ill fortune would be yours if you rushed.

Runestones were carved on large stone slabs that were later erected. Smaller, personal objects were quick and manageable with skill and experience.

To carve horizontal and vertical lines, we used:

Chisels: Easy and cheap to make, chisels were metal sticks. It required a deft and experienced hand or the stone would chip and crack or the wood would split and splinter, causing the wrong indentations. Imagine having to redo a whole project because you chiseled a few runes incorrectly.

Hammer: Wooden or metal hammers were cheap and common tools. The chisel was hit with a hammer to indent the surface. Runemasters had to be careful not to crack the stone or hurt themselves with inaccuracy. Hammers and chisels could break, so they were often repaired or replaced to ensure quality work.

The Ramsund carving in Sweden is thought to have been carved in the

10th century. It isn't a runestone per se because it was found on a flat rock.

The Jelling runestones in Denmark honor two generations of a royal Danish family. One from Gorm the Old, memorializing his wife, and one from his son Harold Bluetooth after Gorems death. Also in Younger Futhark.

The Rök runestone is the best-known. It marks the beginning of Swedish literature with tautological poetry (statements that tell of ideas and thoughts).

The Einang runestone was part of a church in Norway.

Over 30 Varangian runestones are in Scandinavia and Europe. They describe Varangian guard voyages from the east to Russia, the Baltic, Greece, and Italy.

The placement of runestones in Eastern and Western Europe is like a dotted map, showing how far their reach went—to the Baltic lands near waterways or to towns in Southern Europe.

The Stones

Professional carvers followed a basic layout: the commissioner's name, the name of the person who died and what they accomplished, a prayer, and the carver's name. This shows that rune carvers were literate and carved short, to-the-point messages.

Most were carved in Younger Futhark, and each character had many versions.

There are many romantic stories about a lover's death and memory. The runestone raised by Holmgöt attests to his love for his wife and that there was no better farmhand than her. The runestone was placed on his wife's grave.

Runemasters

Runestones depicting daily life were carved by merchants, farmers, and Vikings. Later in the 11th century, professional runemasters carved commissions for families or individuals. The runemasters appointed apprentices to help with commissions because it was a profitable and labor-intensive job. It was difficult to select and carve large stone blocks correctly, so the runemaster needed to be a skilled stonemason.

The Roots of Divination

Asatru is a Norse heathenry revival that focuses on the Norse pantheon and Norse mythology. Unlike Wicca, there's little emphasis on magic.

The Asatru faith is a reconstructed religion that aims to follow the practices and beliefs of ancient Norse heathens.

Magic still has a role in the Asatru faith. Like most heathen and pagan faiths, Asatru adherents believe in magic and the spiritual realm. Only difference is that practicing magic doesn't make you Asatru or require you to perform rituals or commune with the gods.

Using Runes

But magic is still part of the faith, so I wouldn't leave it out. You can use magic or not. I'll cover Asatru magic, focusing on runes. Then I discuss the uses of runes, how to use them, and a beginner's guide to get started.

Magic in Asatru

Because magic isn't important in Asatru doesn't mean it's useless. One of the most popular goddesses, Freya, was a powerful magician whose power enchanted the Aesir.

If you're interested in divination or spells, magic could be an Asatru practice.

Two types of magic will be discussed. seidhr and runes are the first.

Start of Runes

Seidhr

The Asatru faith values seidr magic. It's believed that seidhr was a shamanic practice in ancient Asatru. Spawork or spell work referred to these practices.

seidhr involves going into a trance to communicate with spirits and visit other worlds. By practicing seidr, you can commune with nature's spirits, the Disir, or even your ancestors (Magic, n.d.).

Goddess Freya is a seidhr practitioner revered for her magic knowledge. It's said she taught Odin magic. This trancelike state may have been induced by chanting or singing, elevating the practitioner's spirit.

It is believed that seidhr allows practitioners to discern and alter destiny by directly influencing destiny's web (Seidr, n.d.).

For this, the practitioner must enter a trance and travel in spirit form to complete their tasks. It can be a blessing, a curse, or a prophecy.

Magic is tricky, and while not vital to Asatru, it's not to be trifled with.

Interpreting runes

The Asatru faith uses runes most often for magic. Why runes?

Simply put, runes are alphabetic symbols that form the cosmic language and allow us to interpret cosmic messages. Like I said with seidhr, if you're interested in runes, do more reading and research. The journey to read and interpret runes is difficult and often leads to a deep personal transformation.

You must approach magic with respect, reverence, and caution. Runes can affect our lives and should be treated with respect.

Runes date to the early Bronze Age. The runes we know today originated in the 2nd century B.C.E. among Germanic Teutones (Regarding the Runes, n.d.). These runes resembled the Etruscan alphabet.

In 7, the myth of Odin and his sacrifice to Yggdrasil mentions the origins of runes. After sacrificing himself with his spear, Odin hung from Yggdrasil for nine days and nights, according to myth. In return, he received runic knowledge.

Later, Odin shared the runes with the gods and people. Freya supposedly learned runes from Odin in exchange for seidhr magic.

Runes were used for sorcery and magic in the past (Regarding the Runes, n.d.). They bring luck and protection and were worn as talismans or amulets.

In modern Asatru, runes are used to divine. Runes are a valuable divination tool because they allow the practitioner to commune with the soul's subconscious. Runic practice builds trust and inner strength.

I think it's important to clarify the type of divination runes can help with. Runic divination doesn't give lotto numbers. It shows where you've been and where you're going. Sometimes it can reveal a path you've been looking for.

This interpretation of divination stems from the belief that fate can be examined and interpreted to tell our future. Since our future is determined by our actions, we can change a known future by altering our actions.

To interpret runes, pull out three runes representing the past, present, and future. By looking at these three aspects and how they relate to each other, you can read the future (within reason).

Asatru runic practices use the runic alphabet Elder Futhark. 24 runes are used.

Runes can be used in active magic, but it's less common. One way to practice active rune magic is to carve a bind rune, which combines multiple symbols to produce a desired effect.

Active runic magic uses galdr, or chant magic. I'll focus on runic divination because it's the most common form of magic in Asatru.

Runes meditation is important

Now that you understand runes, let's talk about how they're used. Before we continue, let me say that magic, in any form, is not to be trifled with.

I recommend doing more research first.

This discusses casting runes for divination and rune interpretation.

Runes

The practitioner casts out runes in runic divination. One of the main purposes of runic divination is to help practitioners make life decisions, such as how to handle problems or how to approach certain situations (Tyler, 2015). Simply, runic divination guides.

For beginners, runic divination can be exciting. Indeed, who wouldn't want to see the future? Expectations should be managed. As stated, this magic doesn't give exact answers.

It won't tell if it'll rain tomorrow or if you'll ace a job interview. It guides. This shows possible futures and decision outcomes. All depend on your actions.

Read the runes and interpret them as best you can.

Runes are a great way to access your intuition and inner voice. It's easy to cast runes. Practitioners may follow a pattern or throw randomly, depending on their intent.

Simple casting involves 1 rune pull. This is used if you need a yes/no answer or a preview. One rune each for the past, present, and future is also used. This method can also be used for situation, action, and outcome if you're having a problem.

Traditional runes are cast in threes or odd numbers.

Two main ways to cast runes.

The first is rune-casting on fabric. Look up at the sky as you pick and cast runes (Tyler, 2015). A variant of this method involves casting the runes and only reading the upright ones.

The second method uses a pouch. Think carefully about your question as you hold the pouch in your non-dominant hand. Pull the runes from the pouch with your dominant hand and arrange them to interpret their meaning (Tyler, 2015).

As with tarot cards, the meaning of runes depends on the layout pattern. The 5-run, 7-run, and 24-run layouts are common.

The layout you choose will depend on your question or problem's complexity. More runes are used for harder questions or problems.

For a simple question, use the five-run format. Complex questions may require a seven-run layout. For complex questions or situations, use 24-rune layout.

With more runes cast, there are more answers to interpret. The more runes, the more complex the answer.

Norse magic in daily life

Few can read runes at first. Runic divination is an art that requires time and practice.

Usually, rune sets come with an instruction guide for beginners. There are many books, blogs, and videos on runic divination.

Rune interpretation is a lifetime pursuit. You'll always learn. Asatru is a continuous learning, reading, and knowledge faith. So don't sit down, cast runes, and expect answers.

Even experienced rune casters struggle with interpretation, and it can take weeks to get answers.

If you're into runic divination, be patient. Rune divination is a complicated art that takes time.

Learn Runes

What runes do you need to begin? Why not stone? Wood? or glass? As with most things in Asatru, the runes you use are a matter of personal preference.

Depending on the material, rune sets can be costly.

Once you've practiced runic divination and developed a passion for it, you may want to upgrade. If you're drawn to a particular crystal, consider buying a set.

Choose the material for your runes based on what feels right to you. Runic divination is intuitive, and so is material choice.

How to apply and study runes

You'll need a quiet, clean space to cast your runes. It could be in your bedroom or in the garden if the weather is nice.

Your spot should be clean and quiet.

Meditate before casting. Meditation helps you focus on the reading ahead. It lets you feel your surroundings.

I cover meditation next.

When you're calm and focused, think about the question or decision you need help with. Use this time to commune with the gods or spirits to guide your reading (Tyler, 2015).

Next, spread out your rune cloth and cast. There are many ways to cast runes based on the question or problem.

For beginners, I recommend starting with the one-rune pull. Start with one rune if you're unsure. A single rune can help calm your mind.

When casting, trust your gut. Don't give up if you fail at first. Practice is needed to use runes.

the runemaster's tools

Runes are rune casters' primary tools. There, you can buy or make runes.

Various Runes

If you're new to runes, making your own set can help you remember each symbol. Painting or carving the symbols can be a form of meditation that infuses more energy into your runes.

Depending on your craftiness and handiness, making your own rune sets can be a creative outlet. Creating Elder Futhark runes requires 24 similar-sized objects for rune tiles (25 if you will be including a wyrd rune).

Local craft stores usually have what you need. To do it like the ancient Nords, you can find the materials in your yard.

Buying from a craft store is easier than searching for uniformly shaped pebbles in a stream.

Spirituality increases when runes are made from natural materials. Personal and unique runes will be made. DIY runes have pros and cons.

Pros

It helps you bond with your runes.

It lets you exercise your creativity since you create a unique set of runes.

Buying is more expensive.

Runes DIY

Several shops and websites sell pre-made rune sets. You can buy them if you don't want to make them. Pre-made ones use techniques and materials that are hard to replicate. Replicating them may be difficult if you're not crafty.

Even though these extra items come with the runes, you are not required to use them or follow the instructions for their use. Rune reading techniques vary, and no two casters use the same method.

Pros

offers options

Several beautifully made runes are for sale; some are so unique you can't replicate them.

Always same size and design

Cons

It will be difficult to form a spiritual bond with your new runes.

Materials

Wood nickels, tree branch slices, kiln-fired clay tiles, or aquarium rocks make good runes. Anything small and uniform works.

Runes

Following are suggestions for rune set materials.

Runes can be made from animal bones left in the sun to bleach and dry. If you collect bones, you can use them. With that, you can make runes from animal bones.

When using animal bones, look for thick, dense ones. Thick, dense bones are best for runes. You may discover through research that using femurs makes rune carving easier.

If you're not a collector and just want rune bones, water buffalo bones are ideal. Because commercial ones are made from animals. These bones are Asian dairy and meat farm byproducts.

The cross of deer antlers makes a great rune. It's cool that you don't have to hunt deer for their antlers. In early winter, male deer shed their antlers after rutting season. You'll find deer antlers near tree bases in their woods.

To connect with Stag energy, make runes from deer antlers. Keep them away from your dog, as they resemble dog kibble.

Wood - You can use any kind for your rune set. You can use magical trees like Ash, Elder, and Oak. You're free to pick any wood with personal meaning, like a tree you planted as a child.

If you're using fresh wood from trees, make sure to dry it thoroughly first. You can skip this step if you buy commercially dried wood.

Stone - Heathenry practitioners say any stone rune is modern. Some believe only bones and wood are used to make runes. It's a myth; you can work on anything. If you can engrave your runes, the stone is also good.

Elder Futhark

Wood and bone were probably used because they were easy to find and carve compared to stones. You can use precious or semiprecious gems or pebbles to make runes. Gemstone runes are beautiful and easy to cast due to their heft.

You can add magical gemstones to the runes to boost their power. You can use jasper for courage and hematite for protection.

Runes can be made of air-dried, oven-baked, or kiln-fired clay. Durability is best with kiln-fired tiles. DIY casters use ceramic tiles because they're easy to paint or carve.

Aside from that, this material connects well with Earth. Buy premade ceramic tiles to paint or engrave. Use broken tile or pots. Reshape to your liking.

Glass and pewter runes are hard to find. Glass and pewter beads are hard to paint because their smooth surfaces won't hold the paint.

Runes can be etched (sandblasted or acid etched) or carved. Each method requires special equipment, skill, and steady hands. Despite being difficult to work with, the results will be worth it.

Rune-making pros and cons

Acrylic paint is the only type that can adhere to stone surfaces, so use it if you're using stones. Most runes, especially those in the form of gemstones, are too small for practical rune readers.

If you want your runes to be easy to read and comfortable in your hands, make them 34 to 1 inch in diameter. This size is also good for reading for others.

Runes vary in size and shape, even within a set. Using the blind draw method of rune casting requires that your runes be roughly the same size and shape. It prevents biased draws.

Do you want flat, round, symmetrical, or asymmetrical runes? Round runes feel good in the hands when drawn from a pouch, but they roll too much when cast. If you're setting runes in lines or grids, use tiles or flat circular stones.

If you want to read reversed runes, you must decide. Face-down or upside-down runes have different meanings in reversals. It's hard to tell if a round rune is face down or sideways. Certain runes look the same upside-down or right-side-up. When dealing with such issues, use asymmetrical runes and memorize their right orientation.

Inscribe runes (With Paint And Ink, Carving, Wood Cooking)

You can write Futhark on any medium. However, some are harder than others. Still, they make beautiful, lasting designs.

Some ways to write runes:

Paints/Ink

Paints or ink are used by most DIY rune casters. You must choose the right pigment based on the material.

You can also use ink to write on the stones. It's the easiest and fastest way to make runes, but also the least durable. If you want the writing to last, apply a layer or two of clear varnish.

Carving

If you want something permanent, carve or engrave the Futhark letters into the tiles instead of painting them. These methods require more skill, and if you're inexperienced, you may cut your hands if you're not careful. Even if they aren't perfect, they're better than painted runes. Plus, it will last longer.

Wood-Burning

This method uses a soldering iron or wand. It uses a small electronic heating element over the wood to leave a charred line.Interpreting runes

The Asatru faith uses runes most often for magic. Why runes?

Simply put, runes are alphabetic symbols that form the cosmic language and allow us to interpret cosmic messages. Like I said with seidhr, if you're interested in runes, do more reading and research. The journey to read and interpret runes is difficult and often leads to a deep personal transformation.

You must approach magic with respect, reverence, and caution. Runes can affect our lives and should be treated with respect.

Runes date to the early Bronze Age. The runes we know today originated in the 2nd century B.C.E. among Germanic Teutones (Regarding the Runes, n.d.).

These runes resembled the Etruscan alphabet.

In 7, the myth of Odin and his sacrifice to Yggdrasil mentions the origins of runes. After sacrificing himself with his spear, Odin hung from Yggdrasil for nine days and nights, according to myth. In return, he received runic knowledge.

Later, Odin shared the runes with the gods and people. Freya supposedly learned runes from Odin in exchange for seidhr magic.

Runes were used for sorcery and magic in the past (Regarding the Runes, n.d.). They bring luck and protection and were worn as talismans or amulets.

In modern Asatru, runes are used to divine. Runes are a valuable divination tool because they allow the practitioner to commune with the soul's subconscious. Runic practice builds trust and inner strength.

I think it's important to clarify the type of divination runes can help with. Runic divination doesn't give lotto numbers. It shows where you've been and where you're going. Sometimes it can reveal a path you've been looking for.

This interpretation of divination stems from the belief that fate can be examined and interpreted to tell our future. Since our future is determined by our actions, we can change a known future by altering our actions.

To interpret runes, pull out three runes representing the past, present, and future. By looking at these three aspects

NORSE MAGIC FOR BEGINNERS   157

and how they relate to each other, you can read the future (within reason).

Asatru runic practices use the runic alphabet Elder Futhark. 24 runes are used.

Runes can be used in active magic, but it's less common. One way to practice active rune magic is to carve a bind rune, which combines multiple symbols to produce a desired effect.

Active runic magic uses galdr, or chant magic. I'll focus on runic divination because it's the most common form of magic in Asatru.

Runes meditation is important

Now that you understand runes, let's talk about how they're used. Before we continue, let me say that magic, in any form, is not to be trifled with.

I recommend doing more research first.

This discusses casting runes for divination and rune interpretation.

Runes

The practitioner casts out runes in runic divination. One of the main purposes of runic divination is to help practitioners make life decisions, such as how to handle problems or how to approach certain situations (Tyler, 2015). Simply, runic divination guides.

For beginners, runic divination can be exciting. Indeed, who wouldn't want to see the future? Expectations should be managed. As stated, this magic doesn't give exact answers.

It won't tell if it'll rain tomorrow or if you'll ace a job interview. It guides. This shows possible futures and decision outcomes. All depend on your actions.

Read the runes and interpret them as best you can.

Runes are a great way to access your intuition and inner voice. It's easy to cast runes. Practitioners may follow a pattern or throw randomly, depending on their intent.

Simple casting involves 1 rune pull. This is used if you need a yes/no answer or a preview. One rune each for the past, present, and future is also used. This method can also be used for situation, action, and outcome if you're having a problem.

Traditional runes are cast in threes or odd numbers.

Two main ways to cast runes.

The first is rune-casting on fabric. Look up at the sky as you pick and cast runes (Tyler, 2015). A variant of this method involves casting the runes and only reading the upright ones.

The second method uses a pouch. Think carefully about your question as you hold the pouch in your non-dominant hand. Pull the runes from the pouch with your dominant hand and arrange them to interpret their meaning (Tyler, 2015).

As with tarot cards, the meaning of runes depends on the layout pattern. The 5-run, 7-run, and 24-run layouts are common.

The layout you choose will depend on your question or problem's complexity. More runes are used for harder questions or problems.

For a simple question, use the five-run format. Complex questions may require a seven-run layout. For complex questions or situations, use 24-rune layout.

With more runes cast, there are more answers to interpret. The more runes, the more complex the answer.

Norse magic in daily life

Few can read runes at first. Runic divination is an art that requires time and practice.

Usually, rune sets come with an instruction guide for beginners. There are many books, blogs, and videos on runic divination.

Rune interpretation is a lifetime pursuit. You'll always learn. Asatru is a continuous learning, reading, and knowledge faith. So don't sit down, cast runes, and expect answers.

Even experienced rune casters struggle with interpretation, and it can take weeks to get answers.

If you're into runic divination, be patient. Rune divination is a complicated art that takes time.

Learn Runes

What runes do you need to begin? Why not stone? Wood? or glass? As with most things in Asatru, the runes you use are a matter of personal preference.

Depending on the material, rune sets can be costly.

Once you've practiced runic divination and developed a passion for it, you may want to upgrade. If you're drawn to a particular crystal, consider buying a set.

Choose the material for your runes based on what feels right to you. Runic divination is intuitive, and so is material choice.

How to apply and study runes

You'll need a quiet, clean space to cast your runes. It could be in your bedroom or in the garden if the weather is nice.

Your spot should be clean and quiet.

Meditate before casting. Meditation helps you focus on the reading ahead. It lets you feel your surroundings.

I cover meditation next.

When you're calm and focused, think about the question or decision you need help with. Use this time to commune with the gods or spirits to guide your reading (Tyler, 2015).

Next, spread out your rune cloth and cast. There are many ways to cast runes based on the question or problem.

For beginners, I recommend starting with the one-rune pull. Start with one rune if you're unsure. A single rune can help calm your mind.

When casting, trust your gut. Don't give up if you fail at first. Practice is needed to use runes.

the runemaster's tools

Runes are rune casters' primary tools. There, you can buy or make runes.

Various Runes

If you're new to runes, making your own set can help you remember each symbol. Painting or carving the symbols can be a form of meditation that infuses more energy into your runes.

Depending on your craftiness and handiness, making your own rune sets can be a creative outlet. Creating Elder Futhark runes requires 24 similar-sized objects for rune tiles (25 if you will be including a wyrd rune).

Local craft stores usually have what you need. To do it like the ancient Nords, you can find the materials in your yard.

Buying from a craft store is easier than searching for uniformly shaped pebbles in a stream.

Spirituality increases when runes are made from natural materials. Personal and unique runes will be made. DIY runes have pros and cons.

Pros

It helps you bond with your runes.

It lets you exercise your creativity since you create a unique set of runes.

Buying is more expensive.

Chapter 6

Runes DIY

Several shops and websites sell pre-made rune sets. You can buy them if you don't want to make them. Pre-made ones use techniques and materials that are hard to replicate. Replicating them may be difficult if you're not crafty.

Even though these extra items come with the runes, you are not required to use them or follow the instructions for their use. Rune reading techniques vary, and no two casters use the same method.

Pros

offers options

Several beautifully made runes are for sale; some are so unique you can't replicate them.

Always same size and design

Cons

It will be difficult to form a spiritual bond with your new runes.

Materials

Wood nickels, tree branch slices, kiln-fired clay tiles, or aquarium rocks make good runes. Anything small and uniform works.

Runes

Following are suggestions for rune set materials.

Runes can be made from animal bones left in the sun to bleach and dry. If you collect bones, you can use them. With that, you can make runes from animal bones.

When using animal bones, look for thick, dense ones. Thick, dense bones are best for runes. You may discover through research that using femurs makes rune carving easier.

If you're not a collector and just want rune bones, water buffalo bones are ideal. Because commercial ones are made from animals. These bones are Asian dairy and meat farm byproducts.

The cross of deer antlers makes a great rune. It's cool that you don't have to hunt deer for their antlers. In early winter, male deer shed their antlers after rutting season. You'll find deer antlers near tree bases in their woods.

To connect with Stag energy, make runes from deer antlers. Keep them away from your dog, as they resemble dog kibble.

Wood - You can use any kind for your rune set. You can use magical trees like Ash, Elder, and Oak. You're free to pick any wood with personal meaning, like a tree you planted as a child.

If you're using fresh wood from trees, make sure to dry it thoroughly first. You can skip this step if you buy commercially dried wood.

Stone - Heathenry practitioners say any stone rune is modern. Some believe only bones and wood are used to make runes. It's a myth; you can work on anything. If you can engrave your runes, the stone is also good.

Elder Futhark

Wood and bone were probably used because they were easy to find and carve compared to stones. You can use precious or semiprecious gems or pebbles to make runes. Gemstone runes are beautiful and easy to cast due to their heft.

You can add magical gemstones to the runes to boost their power. You can use jasper for courage and hematite for protection.

Runes can be made of air-dried, oven-baked, or kiln-fired clay. Durability is best with kiln-fired tiles. DIY casters use ceramic tiles because they're easy to paint or carve.

Aside from that, this material connects well with Earth. Buy premade ceramic tiles to paint or engrave. Use broken tile or pots. Reshape to your liking.

Glass and pewter runes are hard to find. Glass and pewter beads are hard to paint because their smooth surfaces won't hold the paint.

Runes can be etched (sandblasted or acid etched) or carved. Each method requires special equipment, skill, and steady hands. Despite being difficult to work with, the results will be worth it.

Rune-making pros and cons

Acrylic paint is the only type that can adhere to stone surfaces, so use it if you're using stones. Most runes, especially those in the form of gemstones, are too small for practical rune readers.

If you want your runes to be easy to read and comfortable in your hands, make them 34 to 1 inch in diameter. This size is also good for reading for others.

Runes vary in size and shape, even within a set. Using the blind draw method of rune casting requires that your runes be roughly the same size and shape. It prevents biased draws.

Do you want flat, round, symmetrical, or asymmetrical runes? Round runes feel good in the hands when drawn from a pouch, but they roll too much when cast. If you're setting runes in lines or grids, use tiles or flat circular stones.

If you want to read reversed runes, you must decide. Face-down or upside-down runes have different meanings in reversals. It's hard to tell if a round rune is face down or sideways. Certain runes look the same upside-down or right-side-up. When dealing with such issues, use asymmetrical runes and memorize their right orientation.

Inscribe runes (With Paint And Ink, Carving, Wood Cooking)

You can write Futhark on any medium. However, some are harder than others. Still, they make beautiful, lasting designs.

Some ways to write runes:

Paints/Ink

Paints or ink are used by most DIY rune casters. You must choose the right pigment based on the material.

You can also use ink to write on the stones. It's the easiest and fastest way to make runes, but also the least durable. If you want the writing to last, apply a layer or two of clear varnish.

Carving

If you want something permanent, carve or engrave the Futhark letters into the tiles instead of painting them. These methods require more skill, and if you're inexperienced, you may cut your hands if you're not careful. Even if they aren't perfect, they're better than painted runes. Plus, it will last longer.

Wood-Burning

This method uses a soldering iron or wand. It uses a small electronic heating element over the wood to leave a charred line.

The charred line won't come off unless you sand the wood heavily.

This technique can also be used on bone tiles, but it must be done in a well-ventilated area.

Since the mystical properties of runes, such as weather control and talking to the dead, are out of reach for mortals, you can use them for divination. This is rune casting.

Respect Runes

Rune casting is a form of oracular divination in which runes are laid out. You can throw them randomly or in a pattern. People get advice on how to handle their problems or situations. Basically, it helps people make smart decisions.

Like other divination methods, runic answers aren't final. If the runes tell you to change course, do so. You are your own master. The runes are there to help.

Buy Runes

Few can learn rune divination on the first try. You'll need time to master the art. A set of runes comes with an instructional pamphlet on how to interpret them. You can consult books and videos to learn about runes, but they won't be enough.

For many, learning to interpret runes takes a lifetime. But it can be uplifting. If you practice, reading them will get easier over time.

If you have good intuition, reading runes is easier. If you don't know the rune's message, don't worry; it may not be about your current situation. Save as much rune information as possible. Write down the details of your divination, especially the ones you're unsure of, and see if they come in handy later.

Rune casters with years of experience admit they don't always understand the runes they cast. Some wait weeks or months for answers after casting.

Pros and cons of buying runes

Whether you're a beginner or a pro, you've probably tried different techniques to improve your rune reading accuracy. A few of your techniques may have worked, but others failed. You've learned a lot, but your rune reading seems unchanged.

Printed by BoD"in Norderstedt, Germany